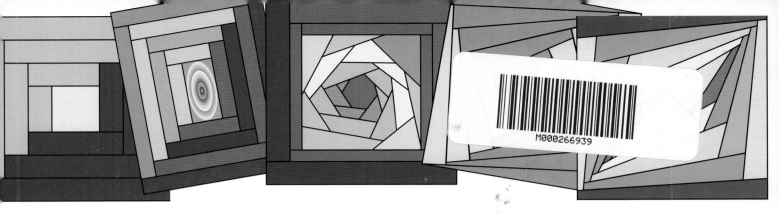

100 ANY-SIZE LOG CABIN BLOCKS

by Linda Causee

Not only is the Log Cabin probably the most popular quilt pattern ever invented, but it has many forms and is completely fascinating in all its forms.

In this book, we've not only shown the traditional pattern, but we have tried to take that basic pattern that has been around for over 100 years and use it as a jumping-off point for some very creative versions. In some cases, the original Log Cabin block is completely discernable; in others, it may be difficult to see the original concept, but the block is still there, constantly inspiring new artists.

Whether you are an experienced quilter or a beginner, you know that one of the most difficult parts of making any quilt is finding the necessary pattern pieces. This book and its enclosed CD will solve that problem. Just select the quilt block you want, place the CD in your computer, click on the desired size (from 2" to 8"), and print out all the templates or paper foundation patterns you need!

LEISURE ARTS, INC.
Little Rock, Arkansas

Produced by

CREATIVE PARTNERS LLC

Production Team

Creative Directors: Jean Leinhauser
and Rita Weiss
Photography: Carol Wilson Mansfield
Book Design: Linda Causee
Technical Editor: Ann Harnden
Pattern Testers: Annabell Acuavera, Joy Davis,
Candy Flory-Barnes, Faith Horsky, Ada
LeClaire, Pat Ludwick, Wanda MacLachlan
Machine Quilter: Faith Horsky

Special Thanks to:
Northcott Silks, Inc. and **Westminister Fibers** for
providing fabrics.

Fairfield Processing Company for providing batting.

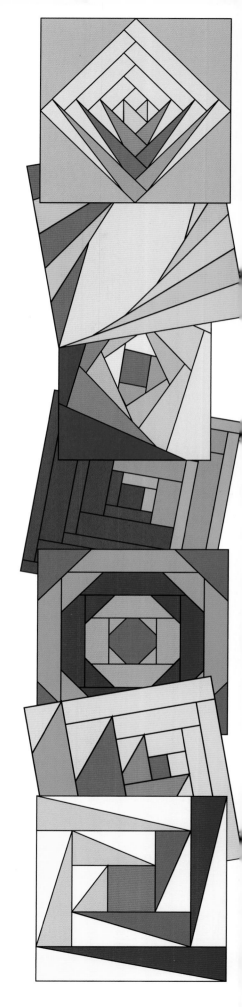

Contents

Before You Start

Choose the block that you want to make. Inside this book, you will find a self-loading CD that contains the 100 quilt block patterns, with each in seven different sizes. The files on the CD are easily opened using Adobe® Reader®. If you don't have Adobe Reader on your computer, you can get a free download at http://www.adobe.com/. The site provides easy, step-by-step instructions for the download.

There are two kinds of blocks in this book: blocks that use templates and blocks that use foundation piecing. For the traditionally pieced blocks, the diagrams are shown broken into separate logs; print the patterns in the size you need and then trace the individual pattern pieces onto template plastic.

For the foundation-pieced blocks, the diagrams are shown as complete blocks; simply choose the size block you want and print out as many copies as you need. If you prefer to use templates instead of foundation piecing, just cut apart the foundation pattern and follow instructions on Making Blocks with Templates on page 67.

If you've forgotten—or if you've never learned—how to make a quilt by either the traditional method or by using the foundation method, we've included some basic directions on page 64. So get ready to make a full-size bed quilt, a wall hanging, or a mini quilt. All of the necessary pattern pieces are just a click away!

Size Guidelines

The blocks on the CD are given as 2″, 3″, 4″, 5″, 6″, 7″, and 8″. If you would like your blocks to be larger, use the following guidelines:

9″ - use 3″ block, enlarge 300%
10″ - use 5″ block, enlarge 200%
11″ - use 3″ block, enlarge 367%
12″ - use 6″ block, enlarge 200%
13″ - use 4″ block, enlarge 325%
14″ - use 7″ block, enlarge 200%
15″ - use 5″ block, enlarge 300%
16″ - use 8″ block, enlarge 200%

Traditional Log Cabin Blocks

Framed Bed Quilt

Chain Linked Wall Hanging

Framed Mini Quilt

Framed Bed Quilt

Size: 81″ x 93″
Block Size: 12″ x 12″ finished
Block #: 5 Framed
Number of Blocks: 30

MATERIALS
2 yards white (includes first border)
2 yards lavender print (includes second border)
2 yards dark pink
1½ yards aqua
3 yards green/aqua (third border, binding)
7½ yards backing
batting

CUTTING
8 strips, 2″-wide, white (first border)
8 strips, 3½″-wide, lavender print (second border)
10 strips, 6½″-wide, green/aqua (third border)
11 strips, 2½″-wide, green/aqua (binding)

Chain Linked Wall Hanging

Size: 42″ x 42″
Block Size: 8″ x 8″ finished
Block #: 4 Chain Linked
Number of Blocks: 16

MATERIALS
½ yard orange
½ yard red (includes second border)
¾ yard blue (includes third border)
1 yard black (includes first border, binding)
1¼ yards backing
batting

CUTTING
4 strips, 1½″-wide, black (first border)
4 strips, 2″-wide, red (second border)
4 strips, 3″-wide, blue (third border)
4 strips, 2½″-wide, black (binding)

Framed Mini Quilt

Size: 13″ x 13″
Block Size: 4″ x 4″ finished
Block #: 5 Framed
Number of Blocks: 4

MATERIALS
fat quarter orange/yellow print (includes second border, binding)
fat quarter gold/light orange
fat quarter brown (includes first border)
fat quarter backing
batting

CUTTING
2 strips, 1″-wide, brown (first border)
2 strips, 2″-wide, orange/yellow print (second border)
4 strips, 2½″-wide, orange/yellow print (binding)

1 Half and Half

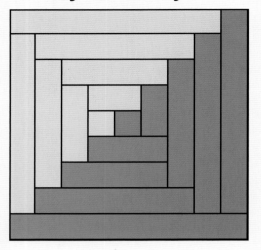

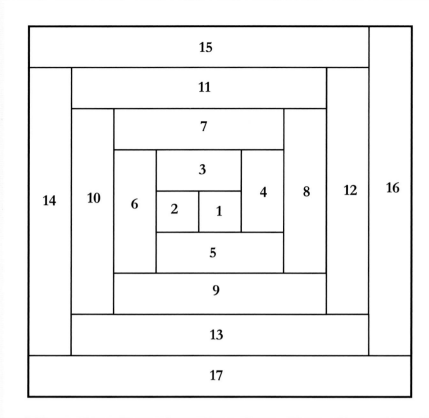

						15					
14	10	6			3		4	8	12	16
			2	1						
				5						
				9						
				13						
				17						

2 Easy Log Cabin

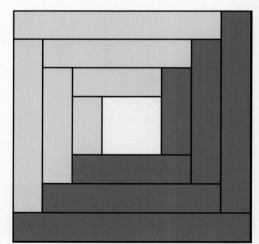

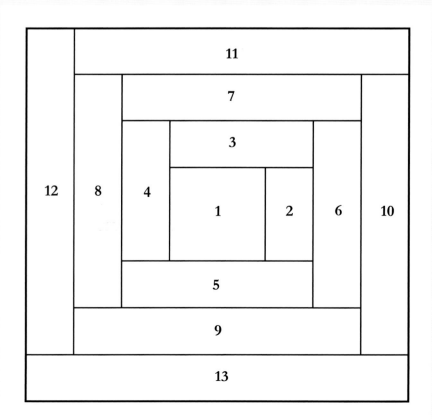

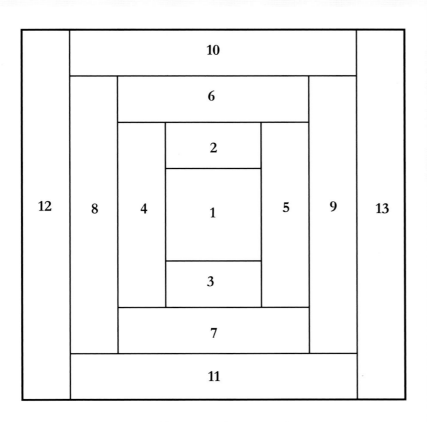

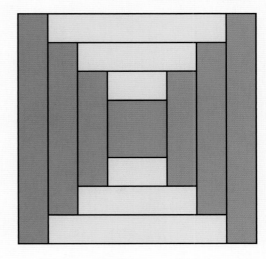

4 Chain Linked

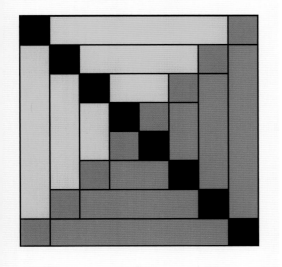

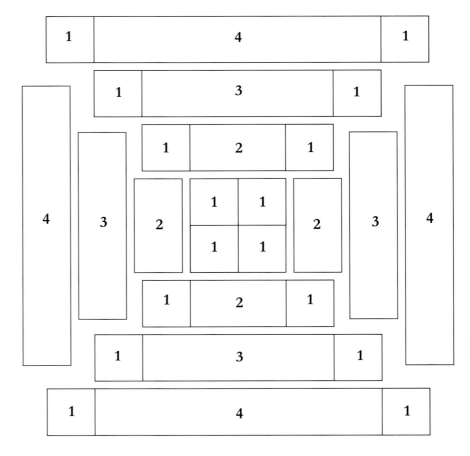

5 Framed

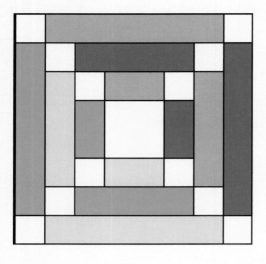

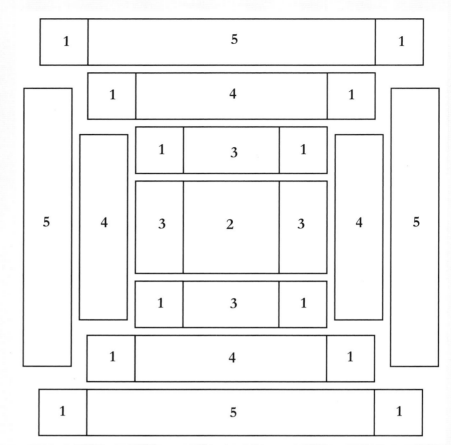

6 Criss Cross

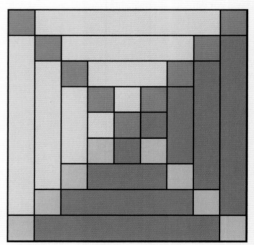

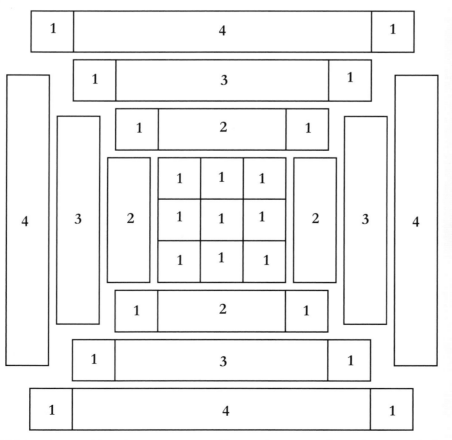

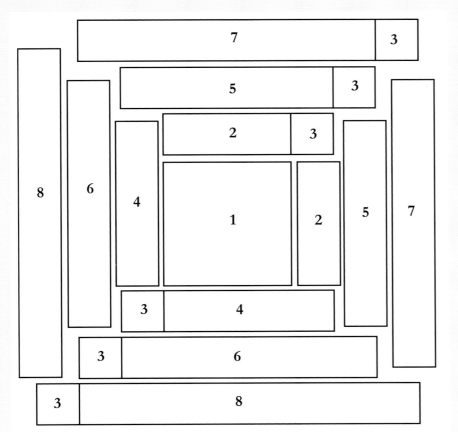

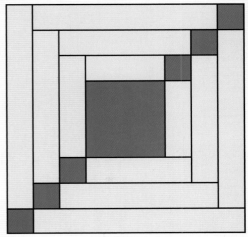

8 Squares in Squares

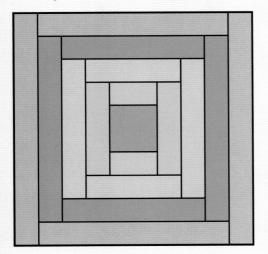

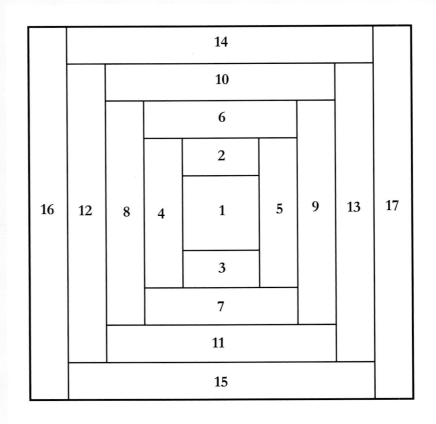

9 Square in a Corner

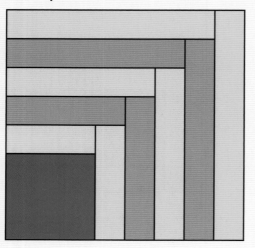

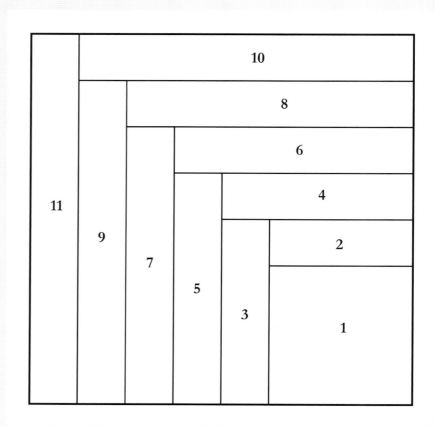

10 Steps to the Top

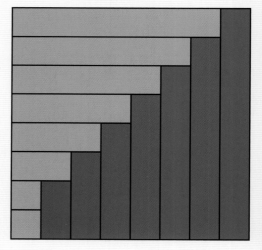

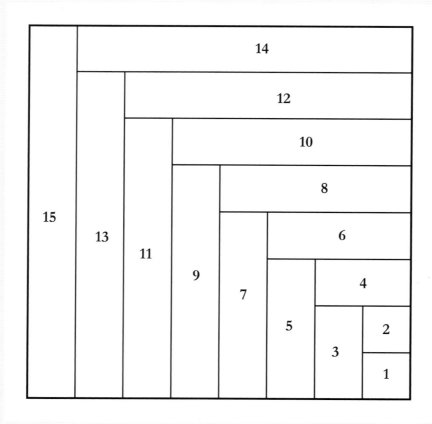

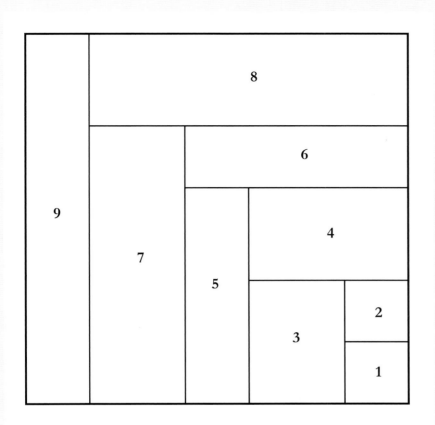

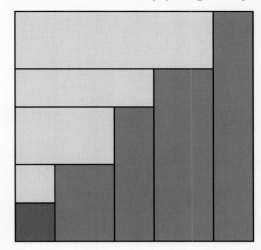

12 *Box in the Middle*

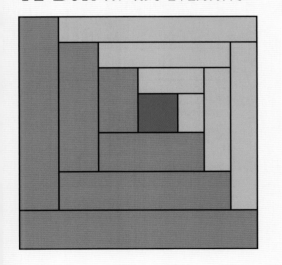

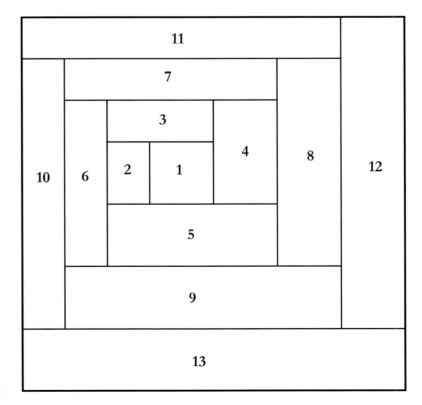

13 Square in a Step

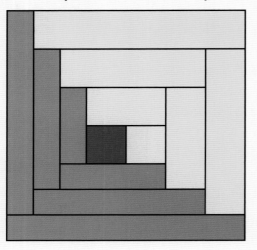

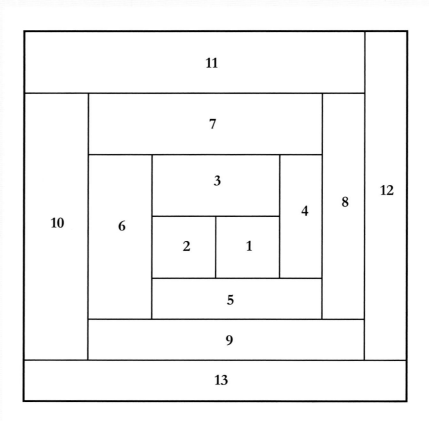

14 Barbell

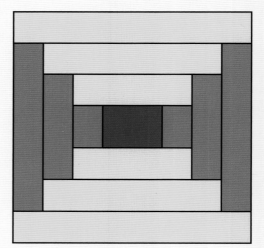

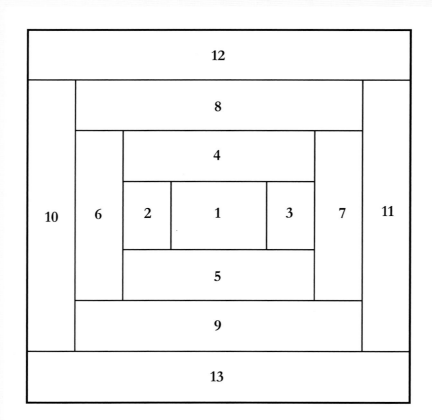

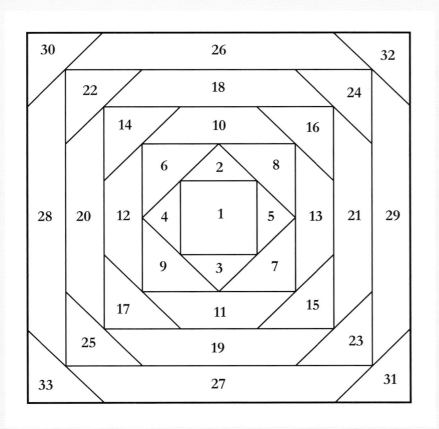

16 Old-Fashioned Log Cabin

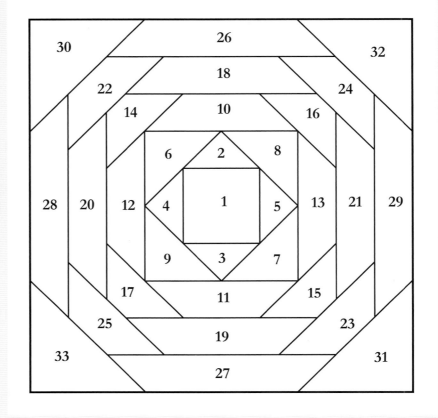

17 Intertwined

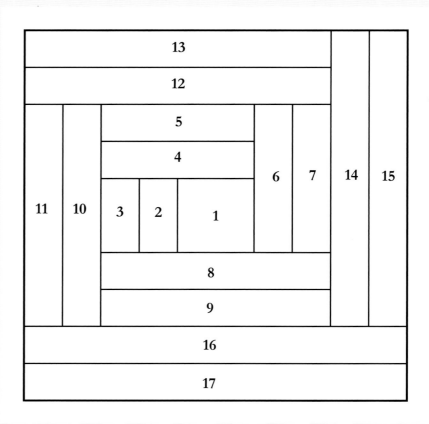

18 Tri-Color Log Cabin

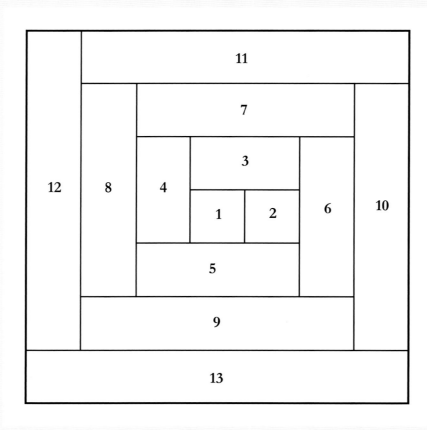

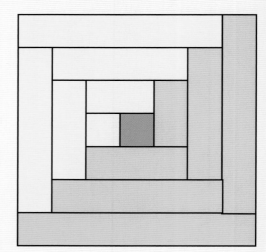

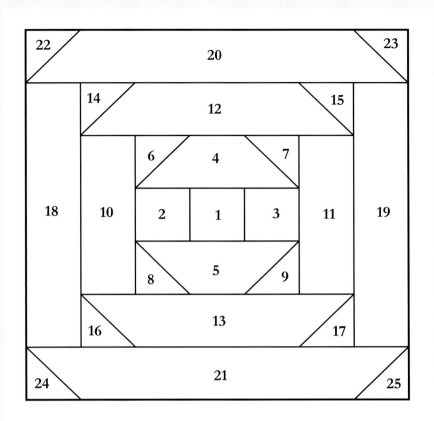

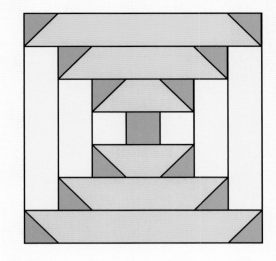

20 Arrows

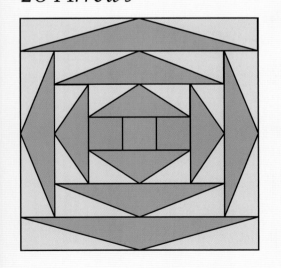

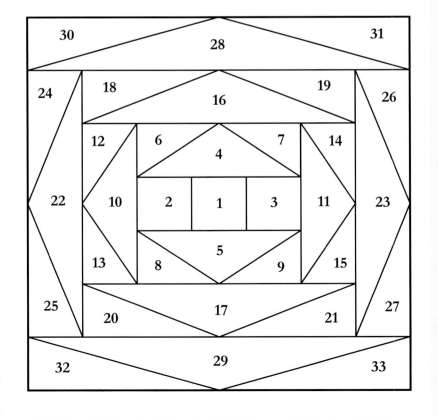

21 Dark and Light

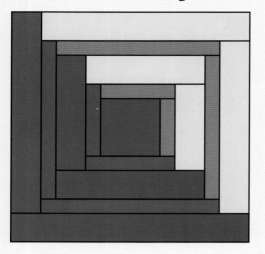

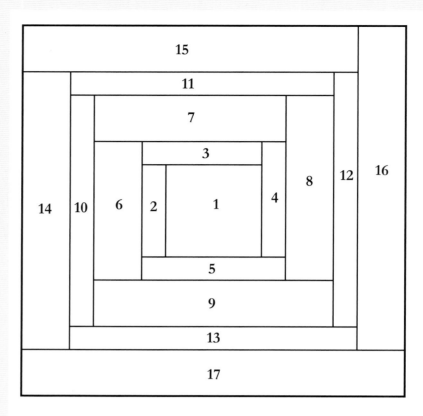

						15				
				11						
14	10	6	2	7	3	1	4	8	12	16
				5						
				9						
				13						
				17						

22 Left and Right

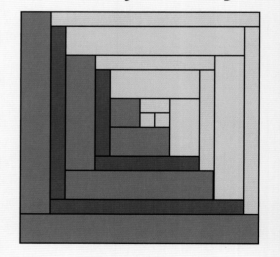

						19					
					15						
				11							
18	14	10	6	7	3 2 1	4	8	12	16	20	
				5							
				9							
				13							
				17							
				21							

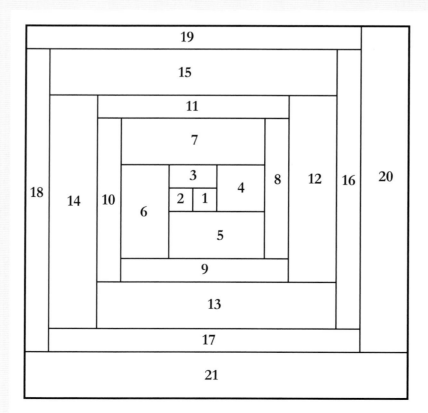

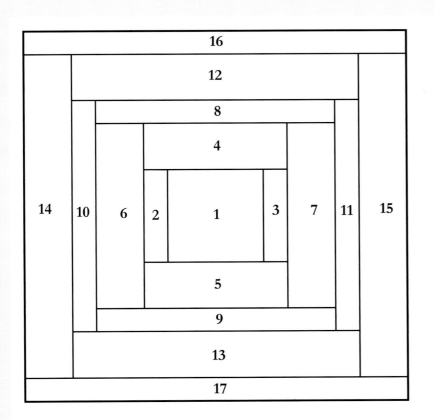

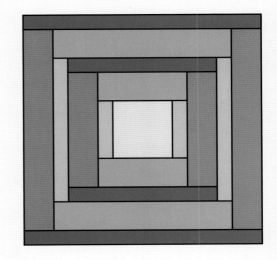

24 *Corners and Stripes*

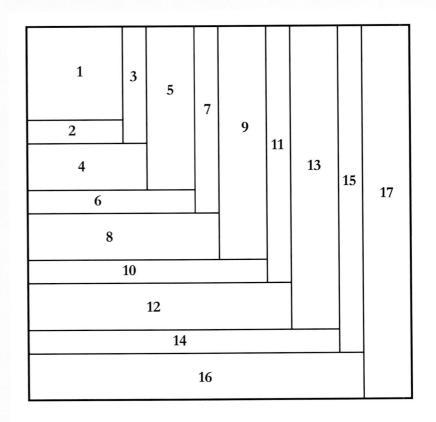

25 Quick and Easy

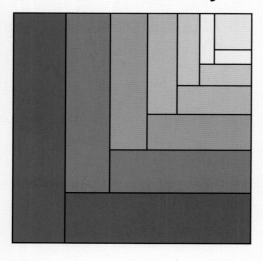

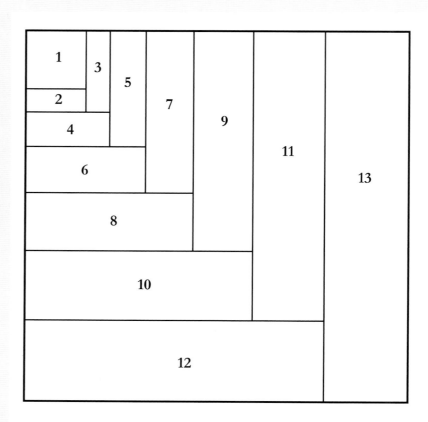

26 Narrow and Wide

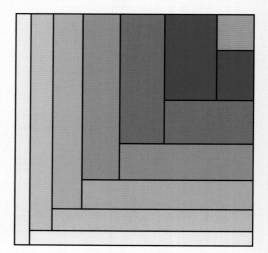

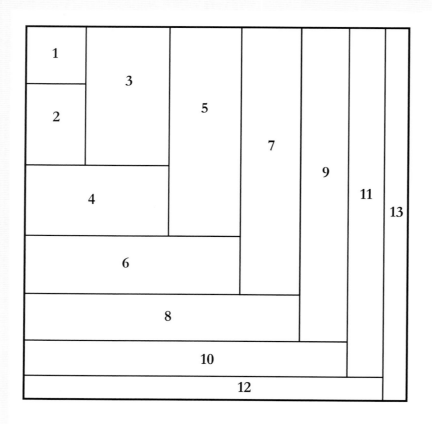

18

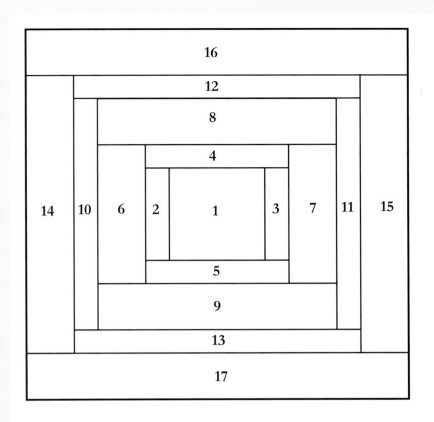

				16			
			12			
			8			
			4			
14	10	6	2	1	3	7	11	15
			5			
			9			
			13			
			17			

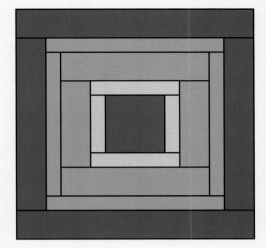

28 *Light and Dark*

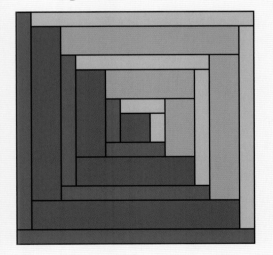

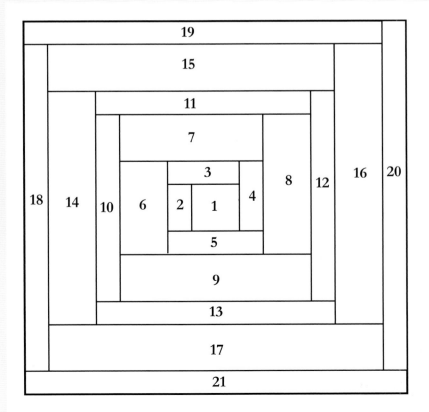

				19			
				15			
				11			
				7			
				3			
18	14	10	6	2	1	4	8	12	16	20
				5			
				9			
				13			
				17			
				21			

Geometric Log Cabin Blocks

Round and Around Bed Quilt

Round and Around Wall Hanging

Round and Around Bed Quilt

Size: 80″ x 104″
Block Size: 10″ x 12″ finished

Block #: 40 Round and Around
Number of Blocks: 42

MATERIALS
2 yards large floral (includes second border, binding)
2 yards white print (includes first border)
2 yards light purple
1 yard light aqua
1 yard med aqua
1 yard light violet
1 yard med violet
1 yard aqua/purple
1 yard teal/purple
1 yard dark purple
6 yards backing
batting

CUTTING
8 strips, 3½″-wide, white print (first border)
9 strips, 7½″-wide, large floral (second border)
10 strips, 2½″-wide, large floral (binding)

Round and Around Wall Hanging

Size: 31″ x 35″
Block Size: 5″ x 6″ finished

Block #: 40 Round and Around
Number of Blocks: 16

MATERIALS
1 yard fall print (includes fourth border)
¼ yard light gold
¼ yard medium gold (includes second border)
½ yard each of light green, medium green (includes third border), orange print, rust print, medium rust print (includes first border), dark rust print and rust/brown print (includes binding)
1⅛ yards backing
batting

CUTTING
*4 strips, 1½″-wide, medium rust print (first border)
*4 strips, 1½″-wide, medium gold (second border)
*4 strips, 1½″-wide, medium green (third border)
4 strips, 3″-wide, fall print (fourth border)
4 strips, 2½″-wide, rust/brown print (binding)
*Sew first, second and third borders together and treat as one border.

Round and Around Mini Quilt

Size: 11½″ x 13″
Block Size: 2½″ x 3″ finished

Block #: 40 Round and Around
Number of Blocks: 9

MATERIALS
fat quarter each of gold, lavender, aqua, green (includes first border, second border, binding)
fat quarter backing
batting

CUTTING
4 strips, 1½″-wide, green (first border)
4 strips, 1½″-wide, lavender (second border)
4 strips, 2½″-wide, lavender (binding)

Round and Around Mini Quilt

29 Sixty Degrees

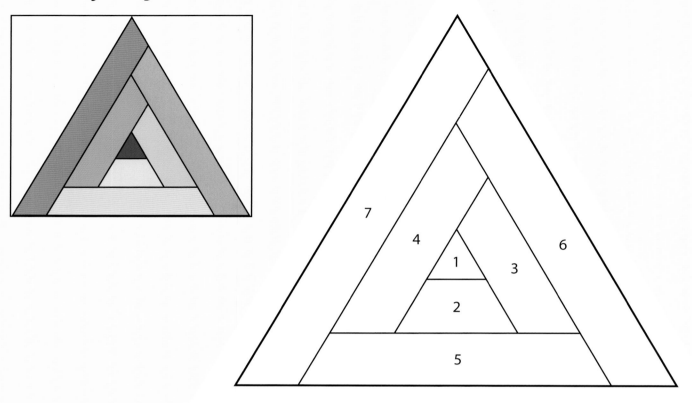

30 Jigsaw Hexagon

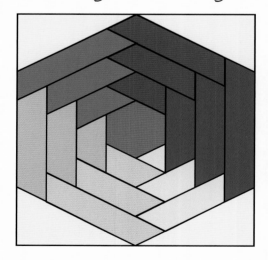

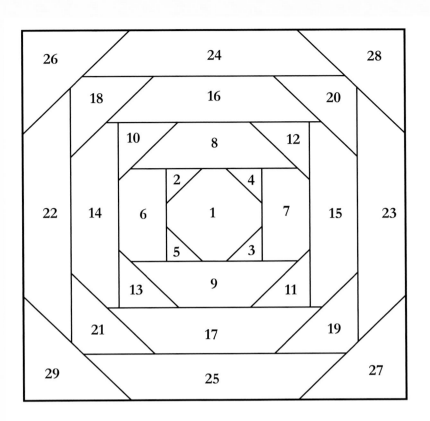

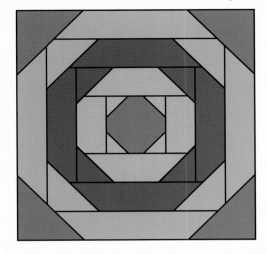

32 *Narrow Steps*

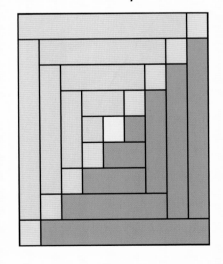

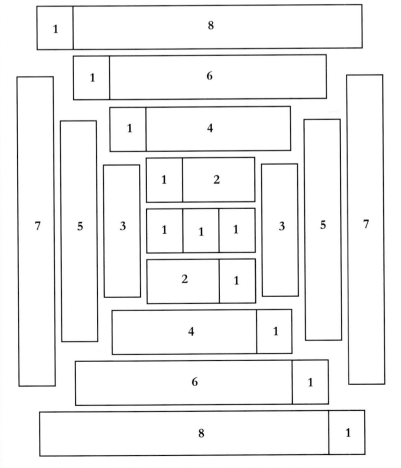

33 Plenty of Points

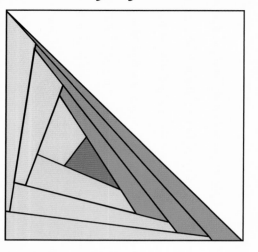

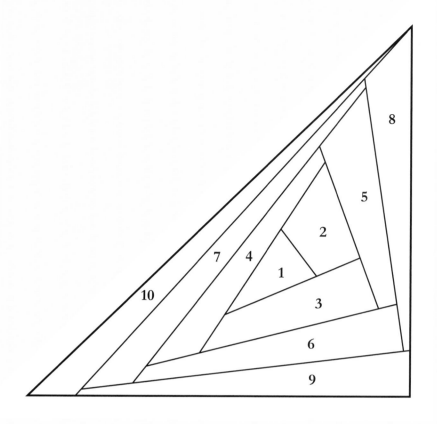

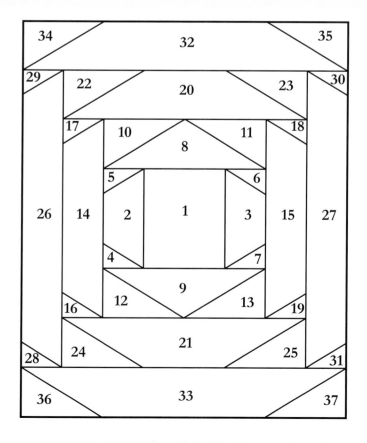

34 Tall Steps

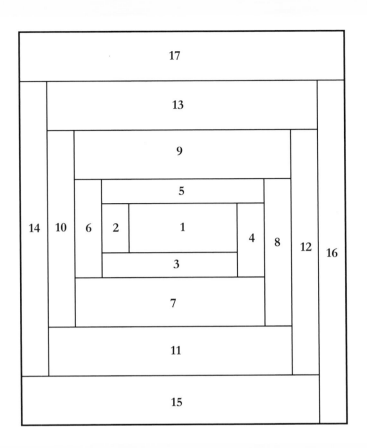

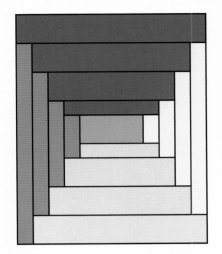

36 *Log Cabin Variation*

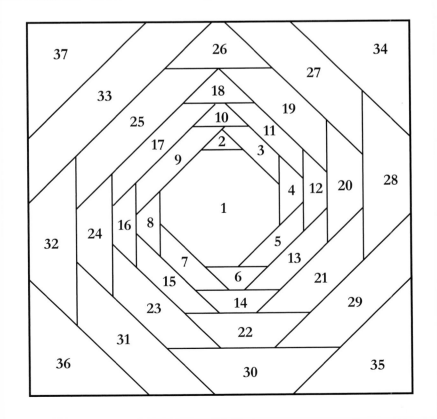

37 Classic Variation

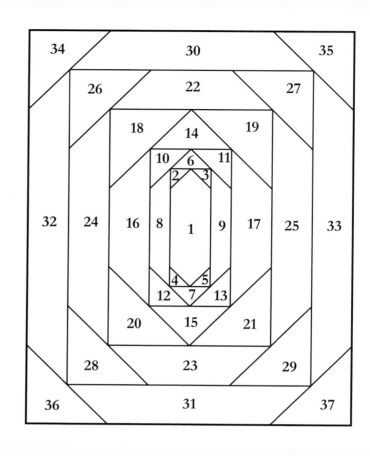

38 Elongated Block

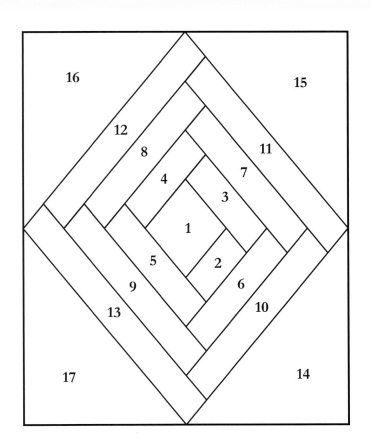

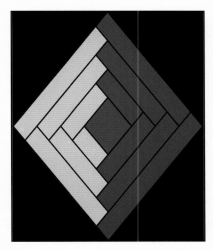

40 Round and Around

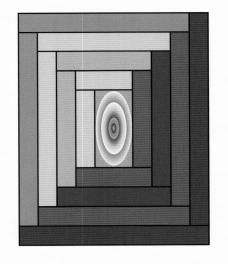

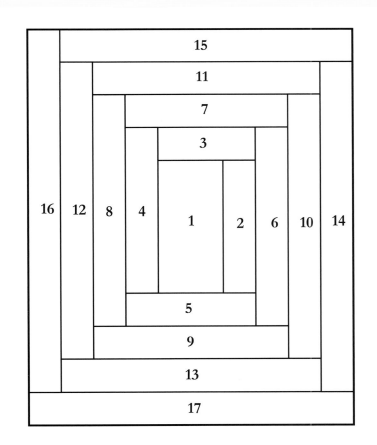

27

41 Log Cabin Triangle

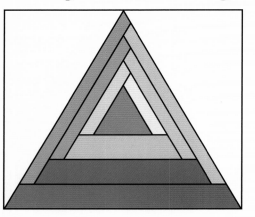

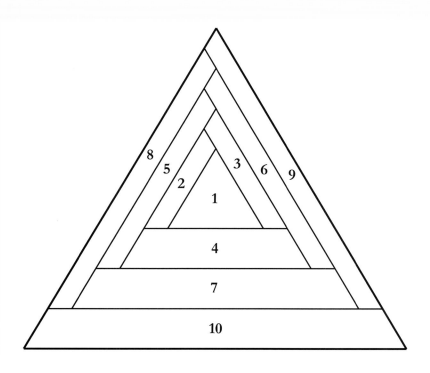

42 Right Angle

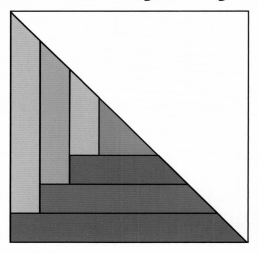

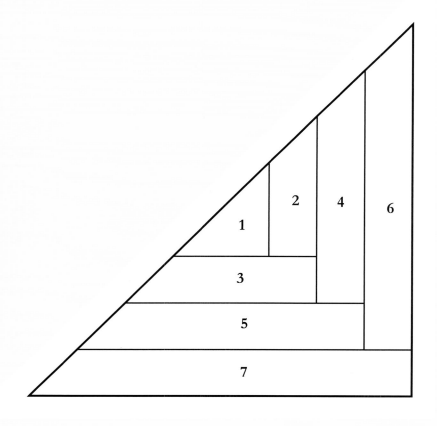

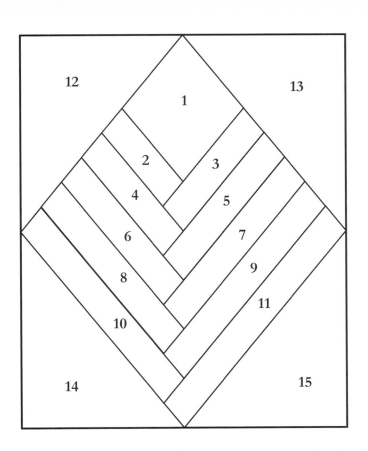

12 13

1

2 3

4

5

6 7

8 9

11

10

14 15

44 *Diamond in the Middle*

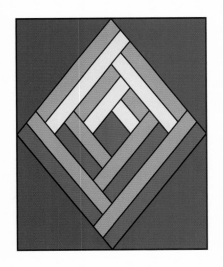

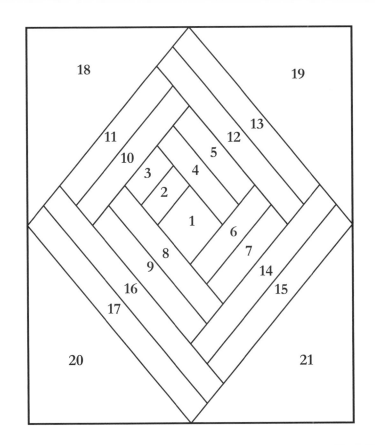

18 19

11 13
10 12
5
3 4
2
1
6
8 7
9 14
16 15
17

20 21

29

45 Pentagon

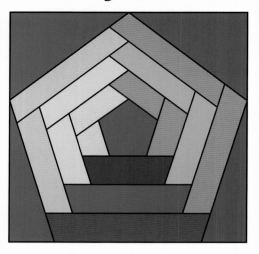

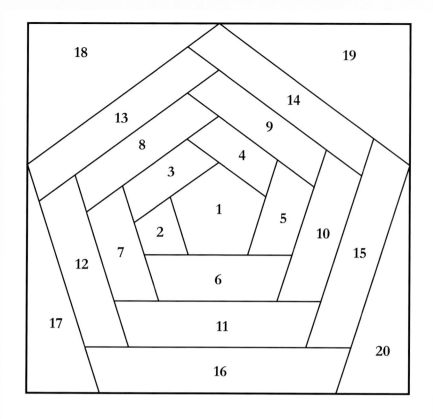

18   19

13   14

8   9

3   4

1

2   5

7   10

12   15

6

17   11

16   20

46 Crazy Pentagon

34   33

26   25

16

27   15

17   6

7   5

18   8   14

1   4   24

9   2   3   13   23

19   10   11   12   22

20   21

29   32

35   30   31

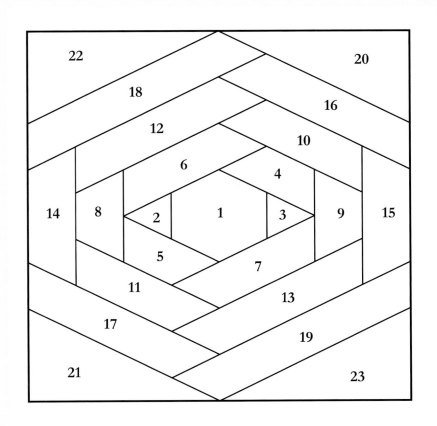

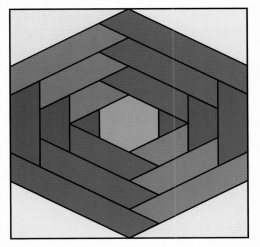

48 Steps Up and Down

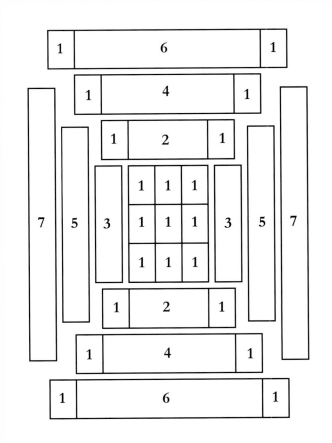

31

Flower Log Cabin Blocks

Crazy Rose Bed Quilt

Crazy Rose Bed Quilt

Size: 78" x 90"
Block Size: 10" x 10" finished

Block #: 50 Crazy Rose
Number of Blocks: 30

MATERIALS
½ yard each of 4 shades (light to dark) of yellow, purple, pink, blue, and peach
½ yard each of 4 shades (light to dark) of green
2 yards off-white (sashing, first border)
1 yard yellow (second border)
2½ yards blue (third border, binding)
7½ yards backing
batting

CUTTING
49 strips, 2½" x 10½", off-white (sashing)
20 squares, 2½" x 2½", assorted pastels (cornerstones)
8 strips, 2½"-wide, off-white (first border)
9 strips, 3½"-wide, yellow (second border)
10 strips, 5½"-wide, blue (third border)
11 strips, 2½"-wide, blue (binding)

Crazy Rose Wall Hanging

Size: 35" x 35"
Block Size: 8" x 8" finished

Block #: 50 Crazy Rose
Number of Blocks: 9

MATERIALS
½ yard each of 4 shades (light to dark) of red
½ yard each of 4 shades (light to dark) of green
½ yard medium green (sashing, first border)
¾ yard red (second border, binding)
1 yard backing
batting

CUTTING
12 strips, 2" x 8½", medium green (sashing)
4 squares, 2" x 2", dark green (cornerstones)
4 strips, 2"-wide, medium green (first border)
4 strips, 3"-wide, red (second border)
4 strips, 2½"-wide, red (binding)

Crazy Rose Mini Quilt

Size: 15¼" x 15¼"
Block Size: 4" x 4" finished

Block #: 50 Crazy Rose
Number of Blocks: 4

MATERIALS
fat quarter each, white, off-white, beige (includes second border), tan
fat quarter each, 4 black prints (includes third border, binding)
fat quarter red (includes sashing, first border)
fat quarter backing
batting

CUTTING
2 strips, 1¼" x 4½", red (sashing)
1 strip, 1¼" x 8¾", red (sashing)
4 strips, 1¼"-wide, red (first border)
4 strips, 1½"-wide, beige (second border)
4 strips, 2"-wide, black (third border)
4 strips, 2½"-wide, black (binding)

Crazy Rose Wall Hanging

Crazy Rose Mini Quilt

49 Tulip

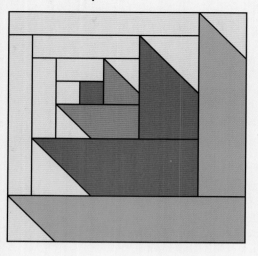

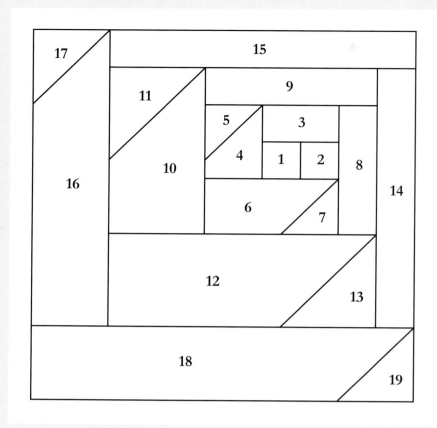

50 Crazy Rose

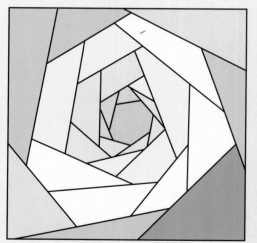

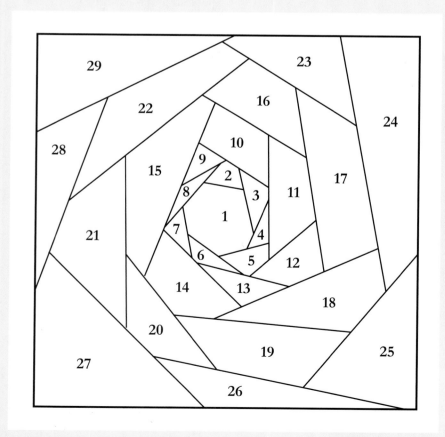

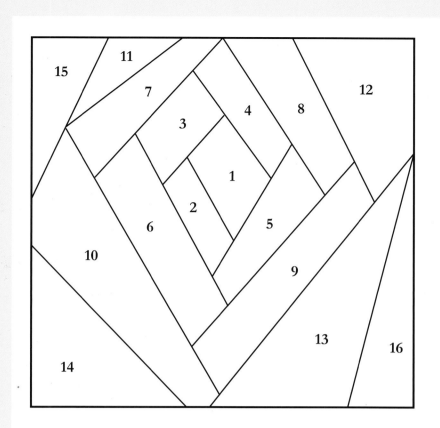

52 Little Tulip

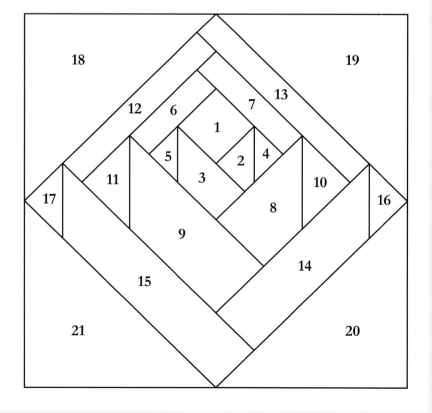

53 Wispy Flower

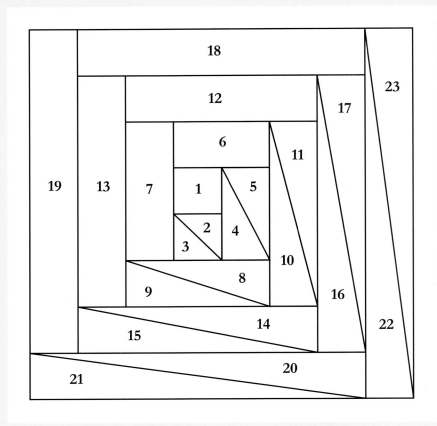

54 Daffodil

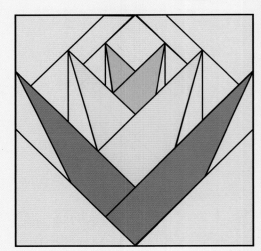

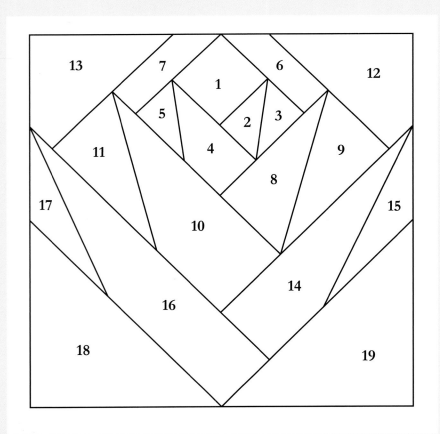

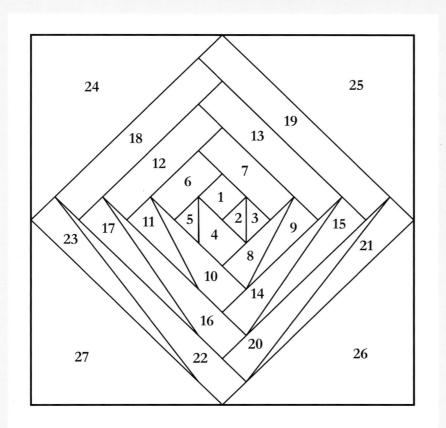

56 Opening Bud

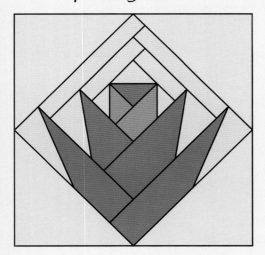

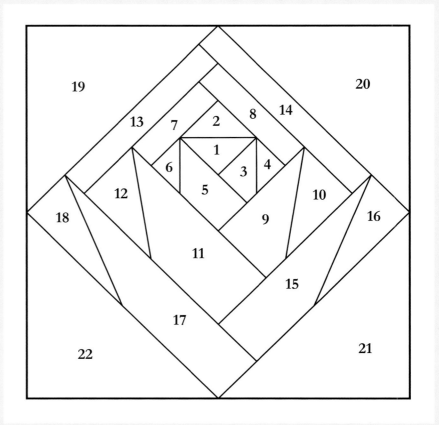

57 Framed Heart Flower

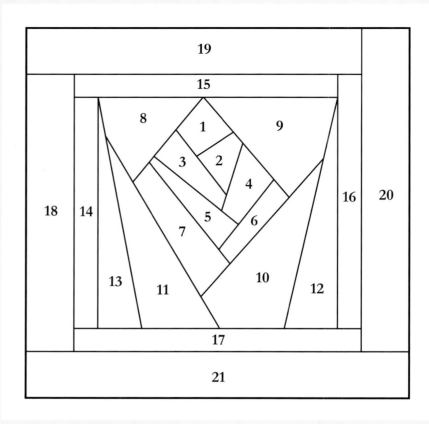

58 Framed Tulip

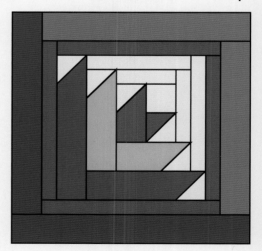

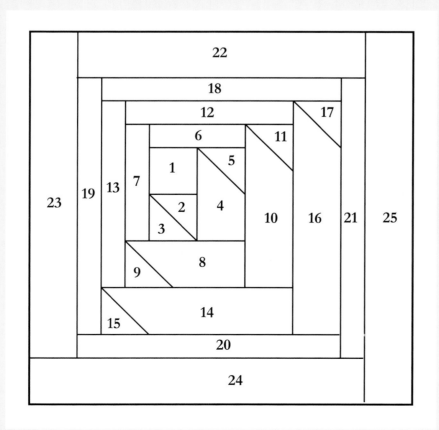

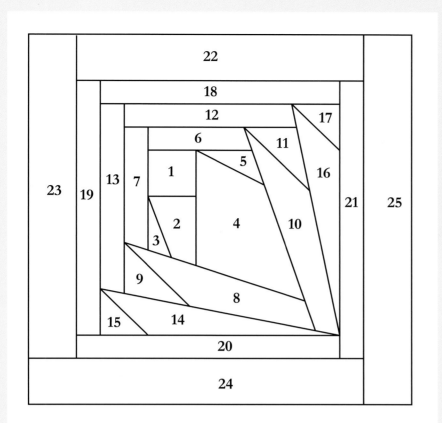

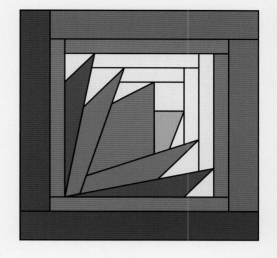

60 Framed Crazy Rose

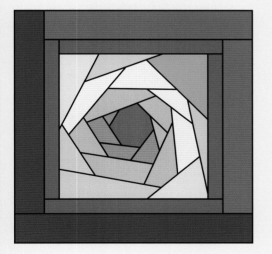

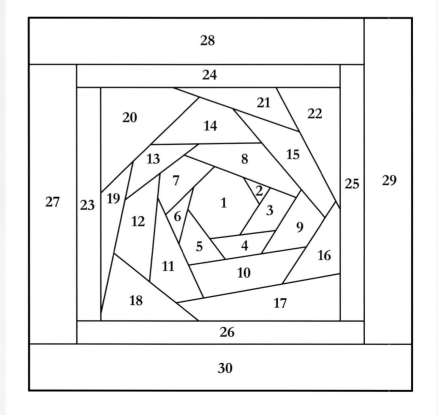

61 Blooming Blossom

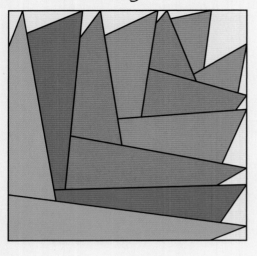

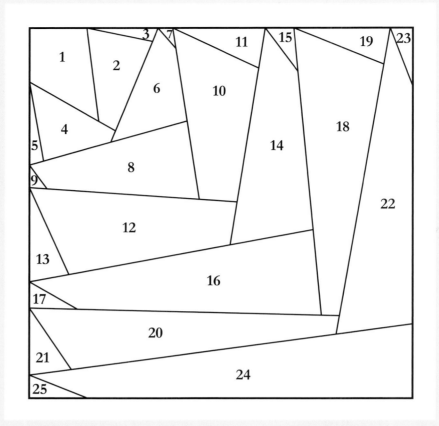

62 Tulip Time

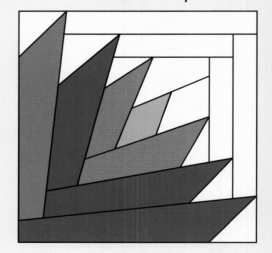

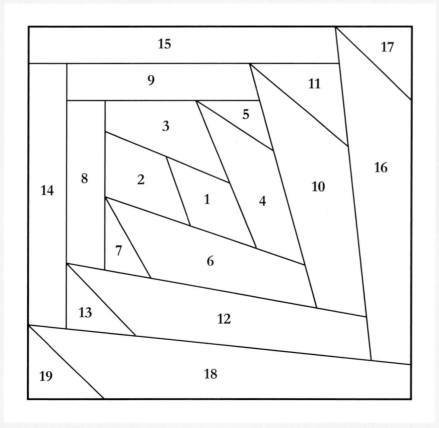

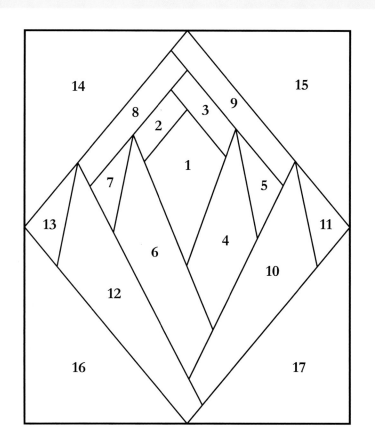

64 Daffodil Patchwork

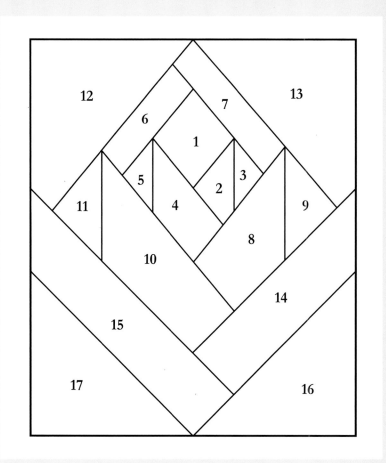

41

65 Blooming Tulip

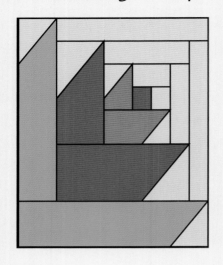

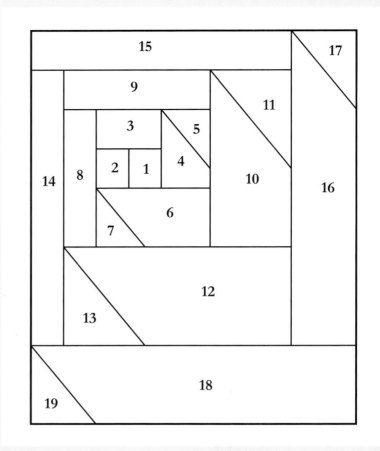

66 Blooming Flower

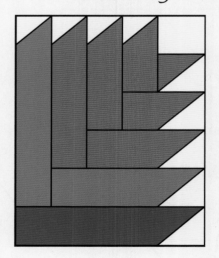

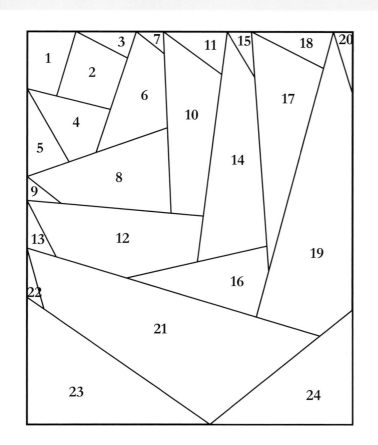

68 Crazy Rose Blooming

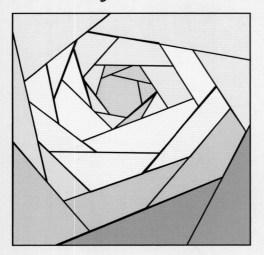

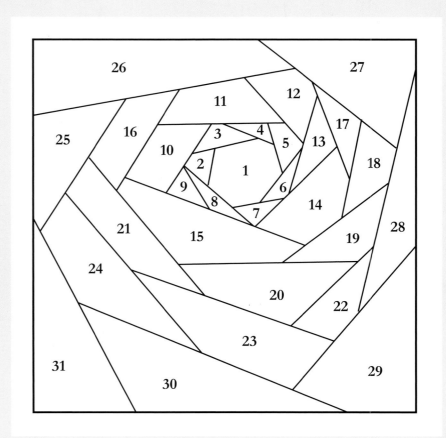

43

Curved Log Cabin Blocks

Pairs of Logs Bed Quilt

Pairs of Logs Lap Quilt

Pairs of Logs Bed Quilt

Size: 84" x 104"　　　　　Block #: 71 Pairs of Logs
Block Size: 10" x 10" finished　Number of Blocks: 48

MATERIALS

3 yards cream
1½ yards peach/tan (includes first border)
2 yards medium blue (includes second border)
2 yards medium rust (includes binding)
1½ yards dark rust
1½ yards dark blue
3½ yards multi-color print (includes third border)
9 yards backing
batting

CUTTING

8 strips, 2½"-wide, peach/tan (first border)
8 strips, 4½"-wide, medium blue (second border)
11 strips, 6½"-wide, multi-color print (third border)
11 strips, 2½"-wide, medium rust (binding)

Pairs of Logs Lap Quilt

Size: 54" x 62"　　　Block #: 71 Pairs of Logs
Block Size: 8" x 8" finished　Number of Blocks: 15 Block A (green)
　　　　　　　　　　　　　　　　　　　15 Block B (tan)

MATERIALS

1 yard off-white
½ yard red (includes first border)
1 yard light green (includes second border, binding)
1 yard medium green
1 yard light tan
1 yard medium tan
1½ yards tan print (third border)
1 yard backing
batting

CUTTING

5 strips, 2"-wide, red (first border)
6 strips, 2½"-wide, light green (second border)
6 strips, 4"-wide, tan print (third border)
7 strips, 2½"-wide, light green (binding)

Pairs of Logs Mini Quilt

Size: 14" x 14"　　　　　Block #: 71 Pairs of Logs
Block Size: 4" x 4" finished　Number of Blocks: 4

MATERIALS

one fat quarter each of white print (includes second border,
binding), medium green print, dark green print, medium red
print, and dark red print (includes first border)
fat quarter backing
batting

CUTTING

4 strips, 1½"-wide, dark red print (first border)
4 strips, 2½"-wide, white print (second border)
4 strips, 2½"-wide, white print (binding)

Pairs of Logs Mini Quilt

69 Whirling Logs

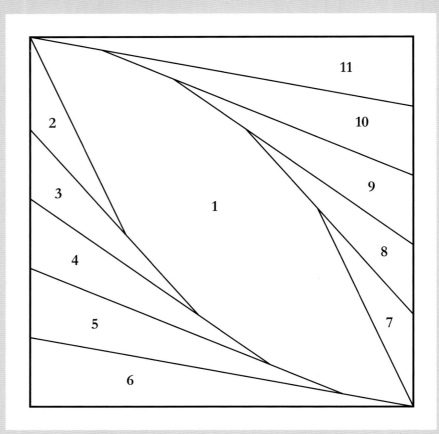

70 Rolling Circle

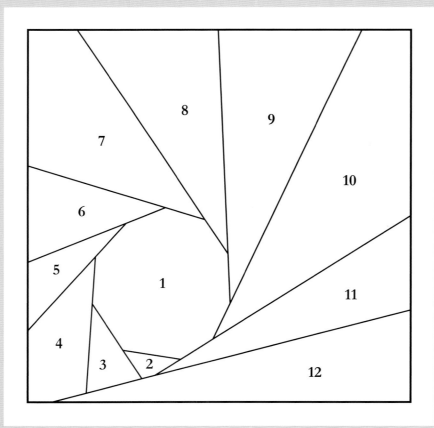

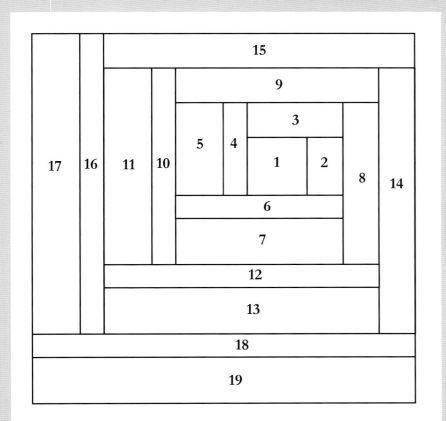

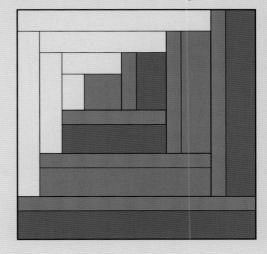

72 *Twists and Turns*

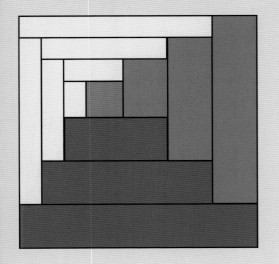

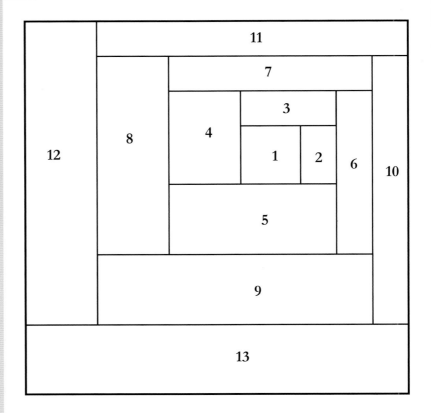

73 Spinning Logs

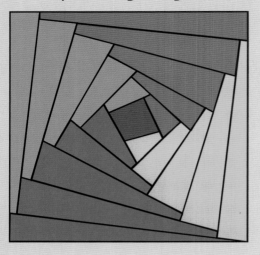

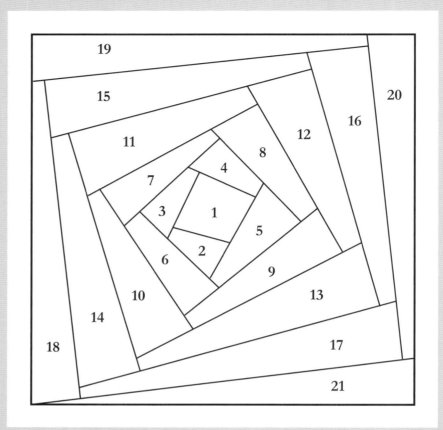

74 Churning Log Cabin

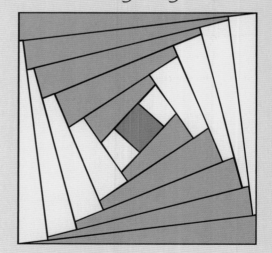

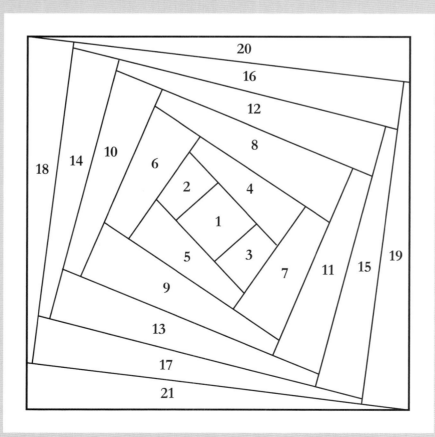

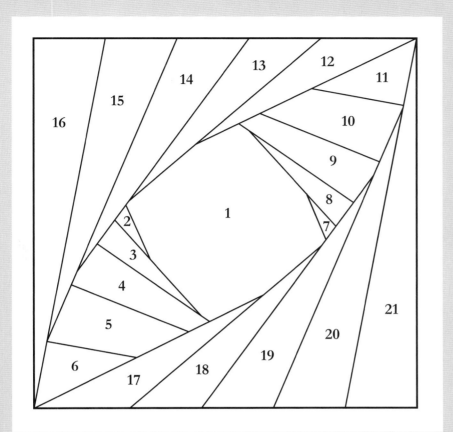

76 Circular Logs

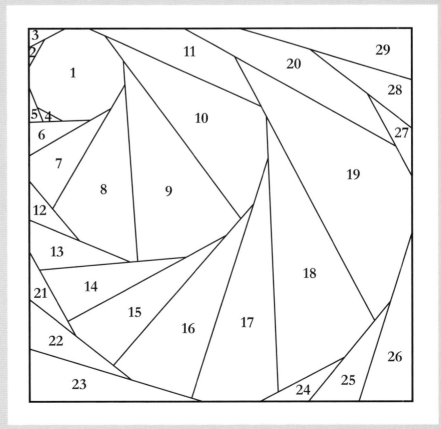

77 Color Burst

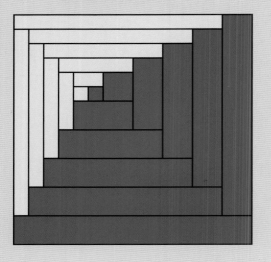

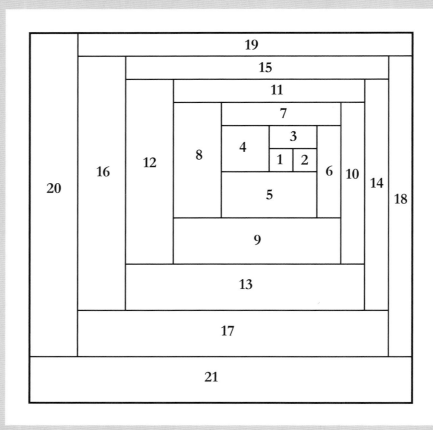

78 Log Cabin Shadow

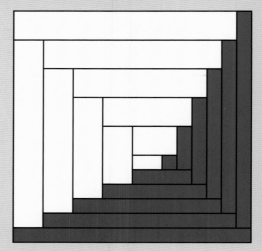

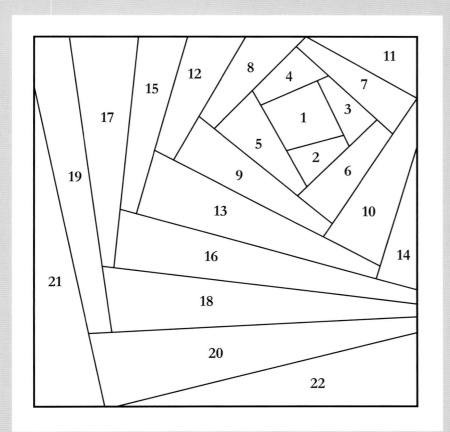

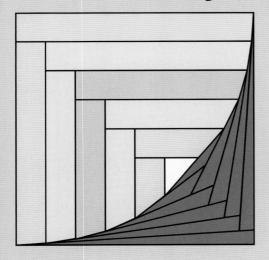

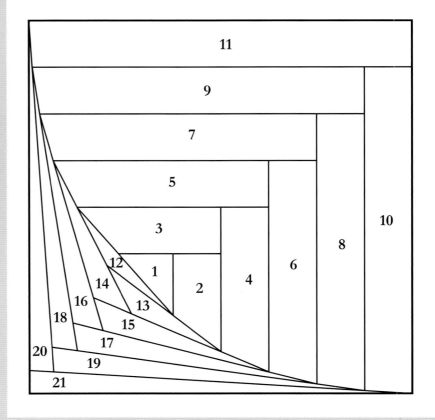

Skewed Log Cabin Blocks

Logs on an Angle Lap Quilt

Logs on an Angle Wall Hanging

Logs on an Angle Lap Quilt

Size: 67" x 75" Block #: 81 Logs on an Angle
Block Size: 8" x 8" finished Number of Blocks: 21 Block A
                                              21 Block B

MATERIALS
1½ yards off-white (includes first border)
1½ yards bright green (second border)
1 yards olive green
1½ yards medium fuchsia (third border)
1 yard dark fuchsia
2 yard large print (fourth border, binding)
5 yards backing
batting

CUTTING
7 strips, 2½"-wide, off-white (first border)
8 strips, 2"-wide, bright green (second border)
8 strips, 2½"-wide, medium fuschia (third border)
8 strips, 4½"-wide, large print (fourth border)
9 strips, 2½"-wide, large print (binding)

Logs on an Angle Wall Hanging

Size: 39" x 39" Block #: 81 Logs on an Angle
Block Size: 6" x 6" finished Number of Blocks: 13 Block A
                                              12 Block B

MATERIALS
1 yard dark rust print (includes first border, binding)
1 yard dark blue (includes second border)
1 yard light blue print (includes third border)
½ yard light rust
½ yard yellow
1⅛ yards backing
batting

CUTTING
4 strips, 1½"-wide, dark rust print (first border)
4 strips, 1½"-wide, dark blue (second border)
4 strips, 3"-wide, light blue print (third border)
4 strips, 2½"-wide, dark rust print (binding)

Logs on an Angle Mini Quilt

Size: 12" x 12" Block #: 81 Logs on an Angle
Block Size: 3" x 3" finished Number of Blocks: 9

MATERIALS
fat quarter yellow print (includes border, binding)
fat quarter each of light aqua, dark aqua, light purple,
  medium purple
fat quarter backing
batting

CUTTING
4 strips, 1½"-wide, yellow print (border)
4 strips, 2½"-wide, yellow print (binding)

Logs on an Angle Mini Quilt

81 Logs on an Angle

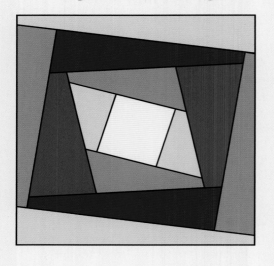

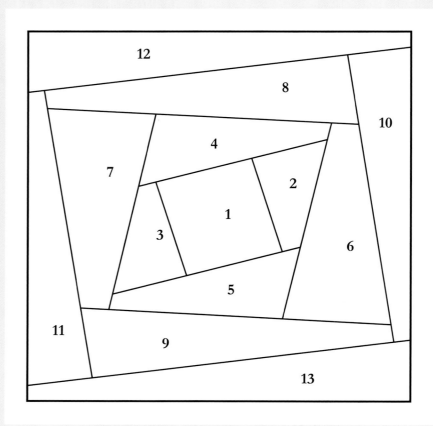

82 Triangles and Squares

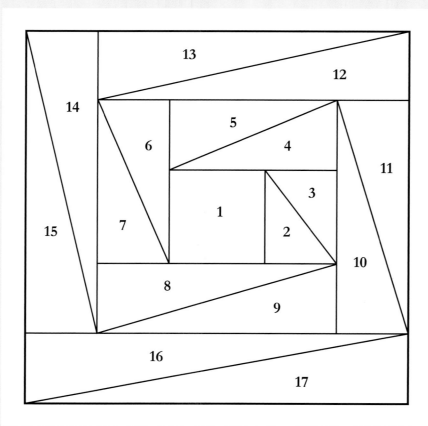

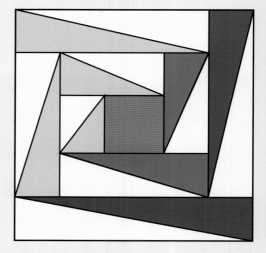

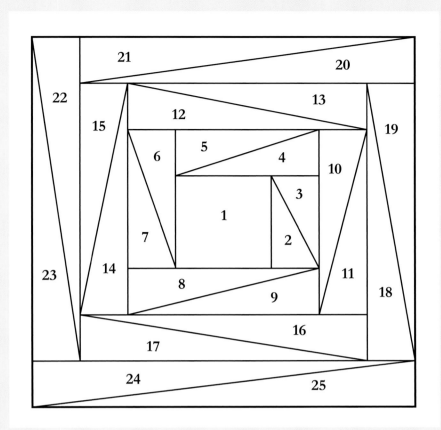

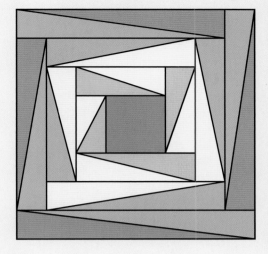

84 Pieces Awry

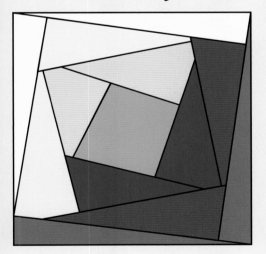

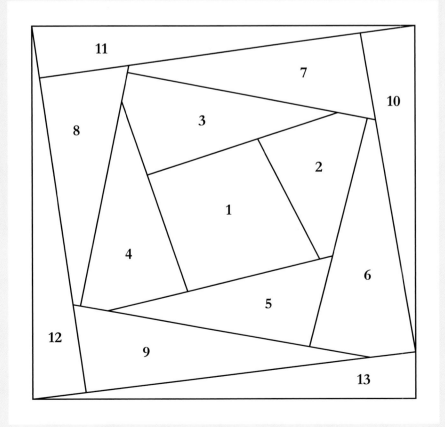

85 Leaning Pieces

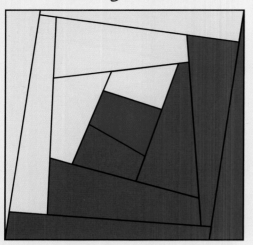

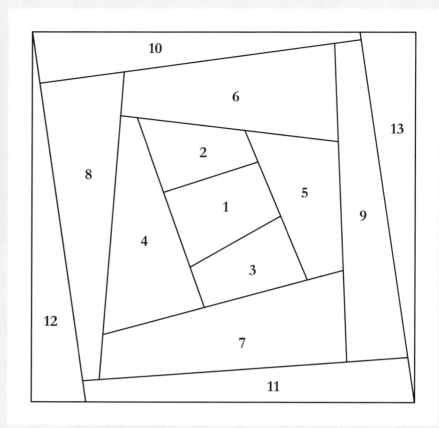

86 Crooked Corners

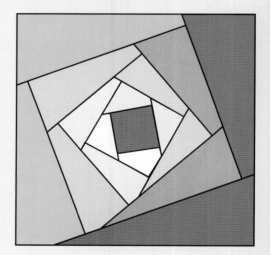

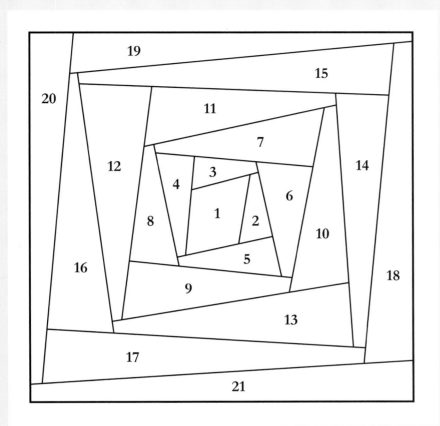

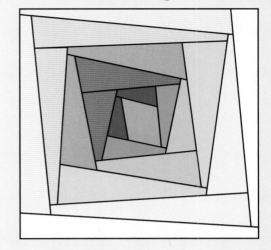

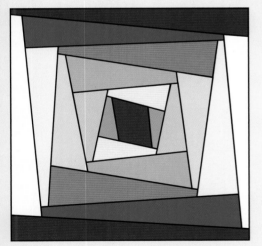

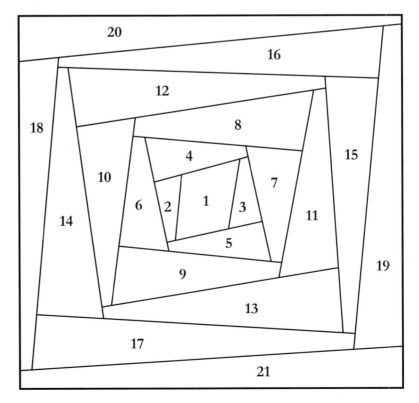

89 Wonky Triangles

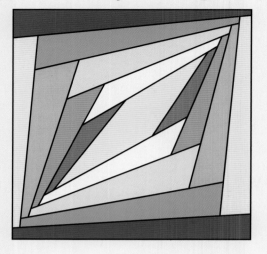

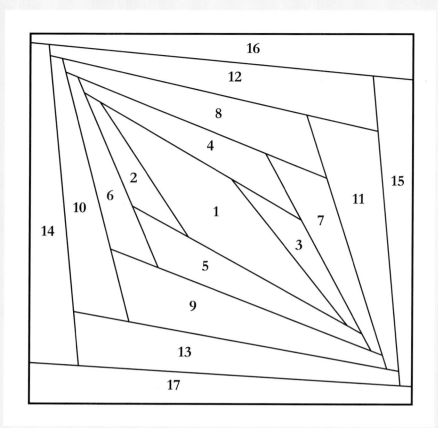

90 Diamond on a Slant

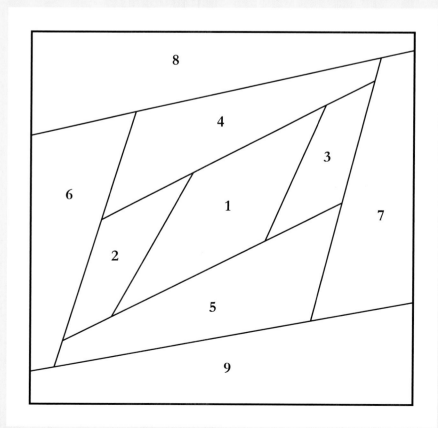

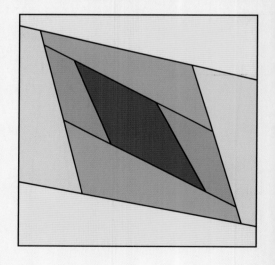

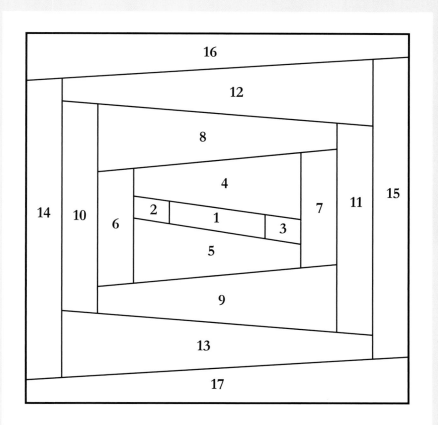

91 Two-Sided Slant

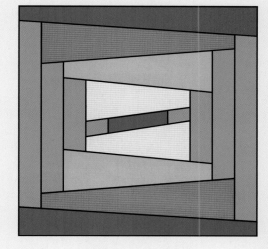

92 Slant Around the Middle

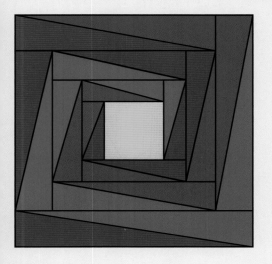

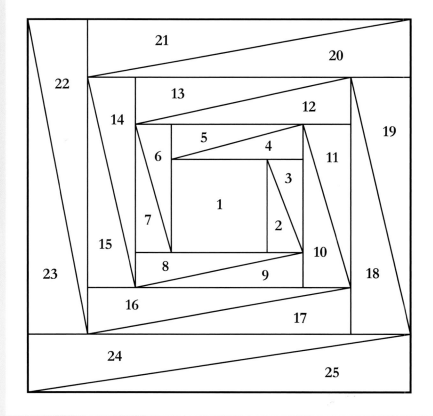

93 Traditional Log with a Slant

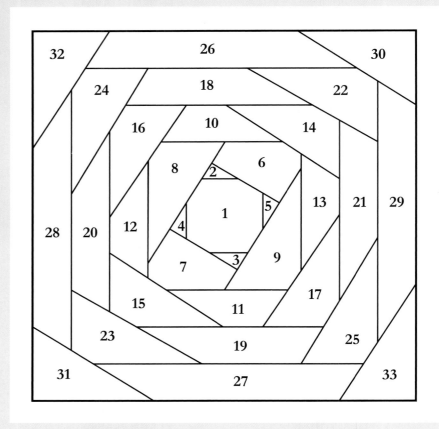

94 Lopsided Center

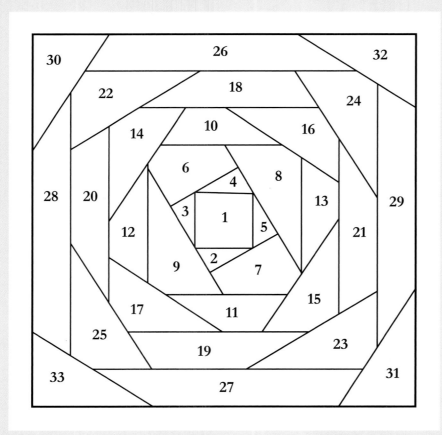

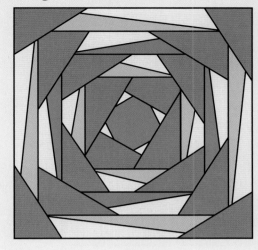

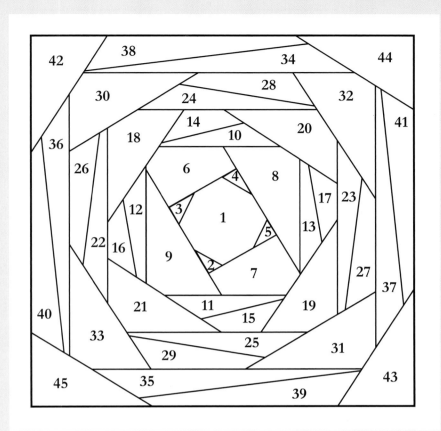

96 *Square in the Middle*

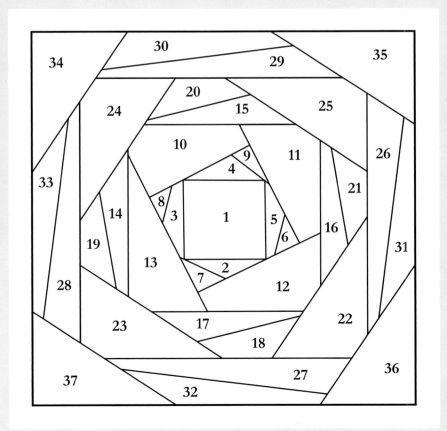

97 Crooked Piece

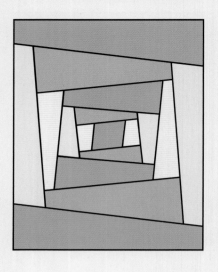

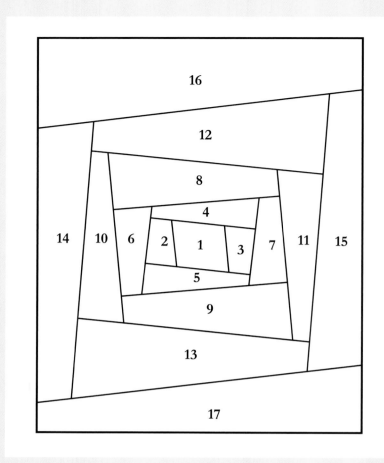

98 Log Cabin Gone Awry

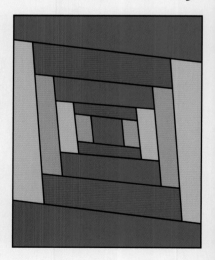

99 *Log Cabin Askew*

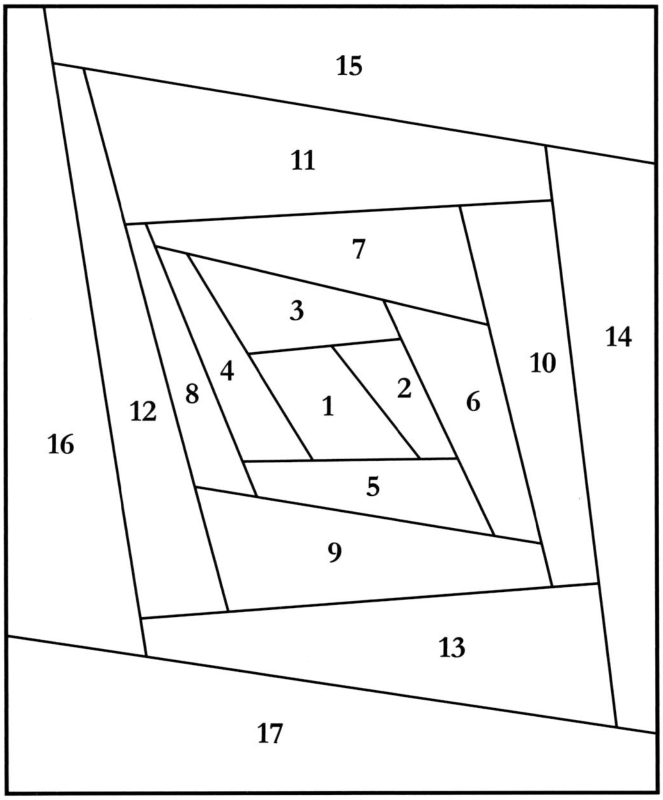
15
11
7
3
14
10
4
2
12
8
1
6
16
5
9
13
17

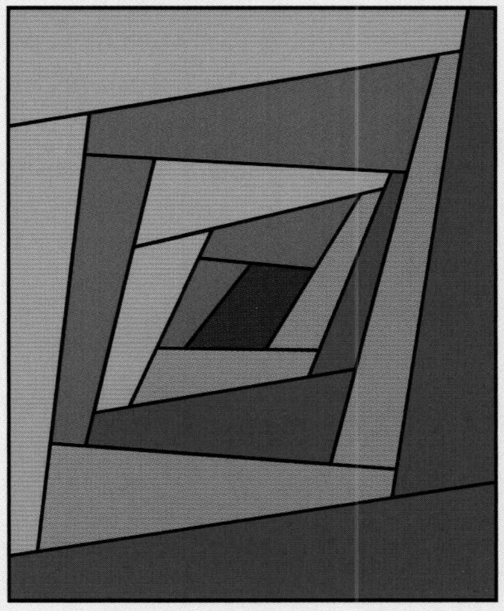

100 *Tumbling Logs*

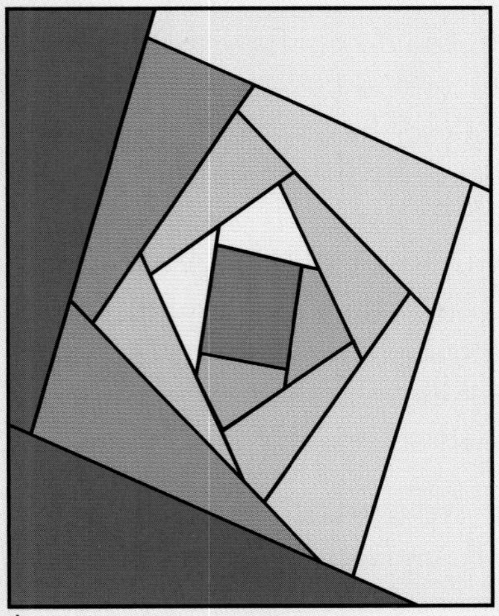

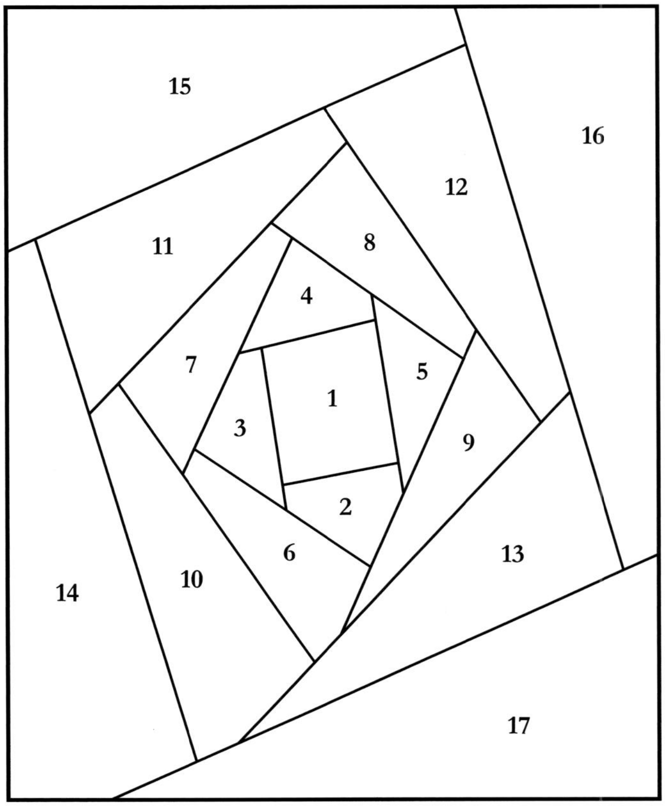
15
16
12
11
8
4
7
5
1
3
9
2
6
13
14
10
17

General Directions

There are two different types of blocks in this book: blocks that use templates and blocks that use foundation piecing. The diagrams given with each block indicate what type of block. For example, diagrams shown as complete blocks, are foundation pieced. **(Diagram 1)**

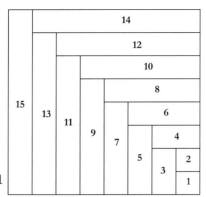

Diagram 1

Blocks that use templates are shown as separate "logs."**(Diagram 2)**

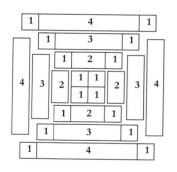 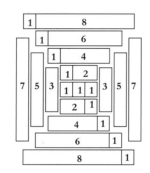

Diagram 2

If you'd like to use templates instead of foundation patterns, just make templates referring to Making Blocks with Templates, page 67.

FOUNDATION PIECING

Materials

Before you begin, decide the kind of foundation on which you are planning to piece the blocks.

Since the blocks in this book are printed from a CD using your computer and printer, the most popular choice for a foundation is regular copy paper since it is readily available. You can also use freezer paper. It comes in sheets by C. Jenkins or a roll by Reynolds®. If you use the roll, you will have to cut sheets that will fit through your printer. If using freezer paper, be sure to print the pattern on the dull side. Then as you piece, use a small craft iron or a travel iron to press fabric pieces in place on the foundation after sewing each seam. The paper is removed once the blocks are completely sewn.

There are other options for foundation materials that can be used with your computer and printer. One type is Tear Away™ or Fun-dation™, translucent non-woven materials, combining the advantages of both paper and fabric. They are easy to see through, and like paper, they can be removed with ease. Another foundation material is one that dissolves in water after use called Dissolve Away Foundation Paper by EZ Quilting®.

Preparing the Foundation

Since the Block Patterns are given in several sizes on a CD, preparing your foundation is easier than ever. All you need to do is decide which block you would like to make (from 2" to 8") and which size you will need for your quilt. Place the CD in your computer, choose the block and print the number of copies that you will need for your quilt.

The blocks on the CD range in size from 2" to 8" since those are the sizes that will fit on a regular sheet of paper. For those that are larger than an 8½" x 11" sheet of paper, you may need to go to your local copier store to print the blocks on 11" x 17" paper. See Frequently Asked Questions on the CD for guidelines on printing blocks over 8" square.

Cutting the Fabric

In foundation piecing, you do not have to cut perfect shapes! You can, therefore, use odd pieces of fabric: squares, strips, and rectangles. The one thing you must remember, however, is that every piece must be at least ¼" larger on all sides than the space it is going to cover. Strips and squares are easy: just measure the length and width of the needed space and add ½" all around. Cut your strip to that measurement. Triangles, however, can be a bit tricky. In that case, measure the widest point of the triangle and cut your fabric about ½" to 1" wider.

Other Supplies for Foundation Piecing

You will need a cleaned and oiled sewing machine, glue stick, pins, paper scissors, fabric scissors, and foundation material.

Before beginning to sew your actual block by machine, determine the proper stitch length. Use a piece of the paper you are planning to use for the foundation and draw a straight line on it. Set your machine so that it sews with a fairly short stitch (about 20 stitches per inch). Sew along the line. If you can tear the paper apart with ease, you are sewing with the right length. You don't want to sew with such a short stitch that the paper falls apart by itself.

Using a Pattern

The numbers on the block show the order in which the pieces are to be placed and sewn on the foundation. It is extremely important that you follow the numbers; otherwise the entire process won't work. When choosing fabrics for your block, refer to the block diagram on the pattern page. **Hint:** *Write your fabric choices on the block pattern to make sewing easier. For example, if you are using red for space 1, write red (or "R") in space 1. Continue for all spaces.*

Making the Block

The important thing to remember about making a foundation block is that the fabric goes on the unmarked side of the foundation while you sew on the printed side. The finished block is a mirror image of the original pattern.

Step 1: Hold the foundation up to a light source—even a window—with the unmarked side facing you. Find the space marked 1 on the unmarked side and put a dab of glue there. Place the fabric right side up on the unmarked side on Space 1, making certain that the fabric overlaps at least 1/4" on all sides of space 1. **(Diagram 3)**

Step 2: Fold the foundation along the line between Space 1 and Space 2. Cut the fabric so that it is 1/4" from the fold. **(Diagram 4)**

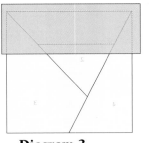

Diagram 3

1/4"

Diagram 4

Step 3: With right sides together, place Fabric Piece 2 on Fabric Piece 1, making sure that the edge of Piece 2 is even with the just-trimmed edge of Piece 1. **(Diagram 5)**

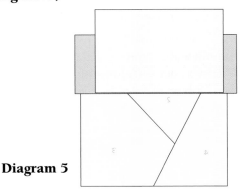

Diagram 5

Step 4: To make certain that Piece 2 will cover Space 2, fold the fabric piece back along the line between Space 1 and Space 2. **(Diagram 6)**

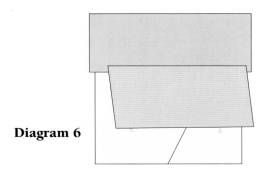

Diagram 6

Step 5: With the marked side of the foundation facing up, place the piece on the sewing machine (or sew by hand), holding both Piece 1 and Piece 2 in place. Sew along the line between Space 1 and Space 2. **(Diagram 7)**

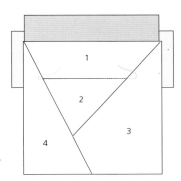

Diagram 7

Hint: *If you use a small stitch, it will be easier to remove the paper later. Start stitching about two or three stitches before the beginning of the line and end your sewing two or three stitches beyond the line, allowing the stitches to be held in place by the next round of stitching rather than by backstitching.*

Step 6: Turn the work over and open Piece 2; press open. **(Diagram 8)**

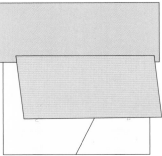

Diagram 8

65

Step 7: Turning the work so that the marked side is on top, fold the foundation forward along the line between Space 1+2 and Space 3. Trim about ⅛″ to ¼″ from the fold. It is easier to trim the fabric if you pull the paper away from the stitching. If you use fabric as your foundation, fold the fabric forward as far as it will go and then start to trim. **(Diagram 9)**

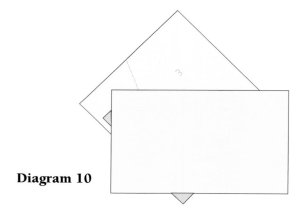

Diagram 9

Step 8: Place Fabric Piece 3 right side down even with the just-trimmed edge. **(Diagram 10)**

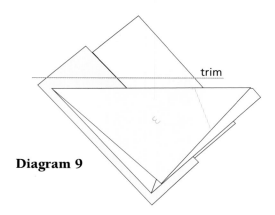

Diagram 10

Step 9: Turn the block over to the marked side and sew along the line between Space 1+2 and Space 3. **(Diagram 11)**

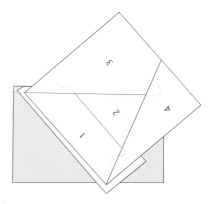

Diagram 11

Step 10: Turn the work over, open Piece 3 and press open. **(Diagram 12)**

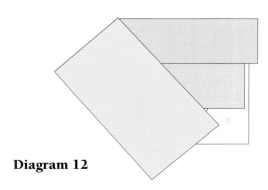

Diagram 12

Step 11: In the same way you have added the other pieces, add Piece #4 to complete this block. Trim the fabric 1/4″ from the edge of the foundation. The foundation-pieced block is completed. **(Diagram 13)**

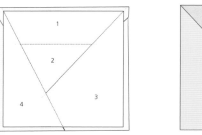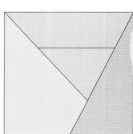

Diagram 13

Note: *The finished block is a mirror image to the pattern used to complete the sewing.*

After you have finished sewing a block, don't immediately remove the paper. Since you are often piecing with tiny bits of fabric, grainline is not a factor. Therefore, some of the pieces may have been cut on the bias and may have a tendency to stretch. You can eliminate any problem with distortion by keeping the paper in place until all of the blocks have been sewn together. If, however, you want to remove the paper, stay stitch along the outer edge of the block to help keep the block in shape.

What You Don't Want to Forget

1. If you plan to sew by hand, begin by taking some backstitches that will anchor the thread at the beginning of the line. Then use a backstitch every four or five stitches. End the stitching with a few backstitches.

2. If you plan to sew by machine, start stitching two or three stitches before the start of the stitching line and finish stitching two or three stitches beyond the end.

3. Use a short stitch (about 20 stitches per inch) for paper foundations to make it easier to remove the paper. If the paper falls apart as you sew, your stitches are too short.

4. Press each seam as you finish it.

5. Stitching which goes from a space into another space will not interfere with adding additional fabric pieces.

6. Remember to trim all seam allowances at least ¼".

7. When sewing points, start from the wide end and sew towards the point.

8. Unless you plan to use it only once in the block, it is a good idea to stay away from directional prints in foundation piecing.

9. When cutting pieces for foundation piecing, never worry about the grainline.

10. Always remember to sew on the marked side, placing the fabric on the unmarked side.

11. Follow the numerical order, or it won't work.

12. Once you have finished making a block do not remove the paper until the entire quilt has been finished unless you stay stitch around the outside of the block.

13. Be sure that the ink you use to make your foundation is permanent and will not wash out into your fabric.

Making Blocks with Templates

Some of the blocks are made using templates. They are shown as separate "logs" and squares. **(Diagram 14)**

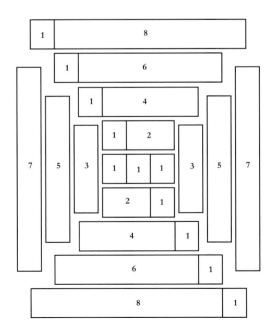

Diagram 14

All you need to do is to decide which block you would like to make. Then, print out the templates of your choice from the CD inside this book.

Note: *If you are machine piecing, add a ¼" seam allowance all the way around the template.*

Then glue the templates onto plastic or heavy cardboard. When you are certain that your glue has dried, cut out your templates. **(Diagram 15)**

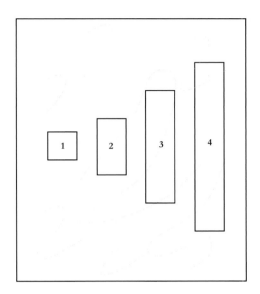

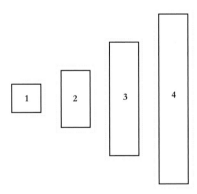

Diagram 15

If your templates become worn, simply repeat the process. The blocks on the CD range in size from 2" to 8" square, which are sizes that will fit on a regular sheet of paper. For those that are larger than an 8½" x 11" sheet of paper, you may need to go to your local copier store to print the blocks on 11" x 17" paper. See Frequently Asked Questions on the CD for guidelines on printing blocks over 8" square.

Cutting and Sewing for Machine Piecing

Lay the template (with the seam allowance already added) on the wrong side of the fabric near the top left edge of the material but not on the selvage, placing it so that as many straight sides of the piece as possible are parallel to the crosswise and lengthwise grain of the fabric. Trace around the template with a marking tool such as a hard lead pencil. This will be your cutting line; use sharp scissors or a rotary cutter and cut accurately.

The traditional seam allowance in quilting is ¼" so be certain that you sew each seam with a ¼" seam allowance. After you have joined two pieces together, press the seams flat to one side, not open.

Cutting and Sewing for Hand Piecing

Lay the template on the fabric as described previously for Machine Piecing and trace around it with your marking tool. This will be your stitching line. **(Diagram 16)**

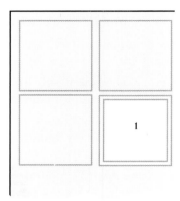

Diagram 16

Now measure ¼" around this shape. Using a ruler draw this second line. This is the line you will cut on. The seam allowance does not have to be perfect as it will not show, but the sewing line must be perfectly straight or the pieces will not fit together.

Hint: *Keep cut pieces in a labeled recloseable plastic bag.*

Sew the number of blocks needed for your quilt.

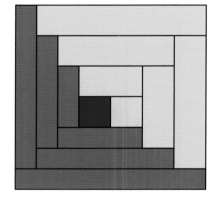

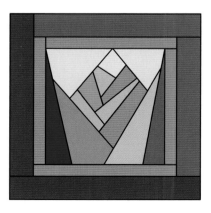

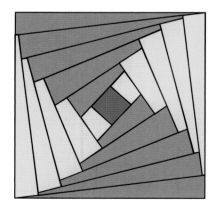

68